Coloring Book for Men

Fish, Fishing Boats, Lures & Tackle

Copyright 2018 Marcia Keszi
All Rights Reserved.

No part of this publication may be reproduced, distributed, or transmitted in any form or by any means, including photocopying, recording, or other electronic or mechanical methods without permission from the author.

Company Name: Marcia K Media Design
website: www.marciakmediadesign.com

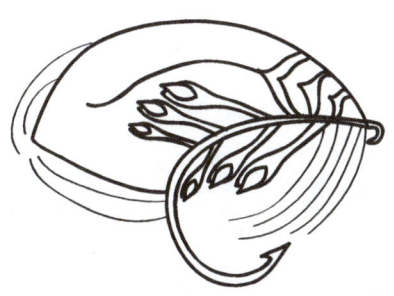

Coloring Book for Kids

Fish, Fishing Tools, Lures & Tackle

Copyright 2018 Marcia Kozai
All Rights Reserved.

No part of this publication may be reproduced or distributed or transmitted in any form or by any means, including photocopying, recording, or other electronic or mechanical methods, without prior written permission from the author.

Company Name: Marcia Kozai Media Design
sbetter/blue.mar.ux.mediadesign.com

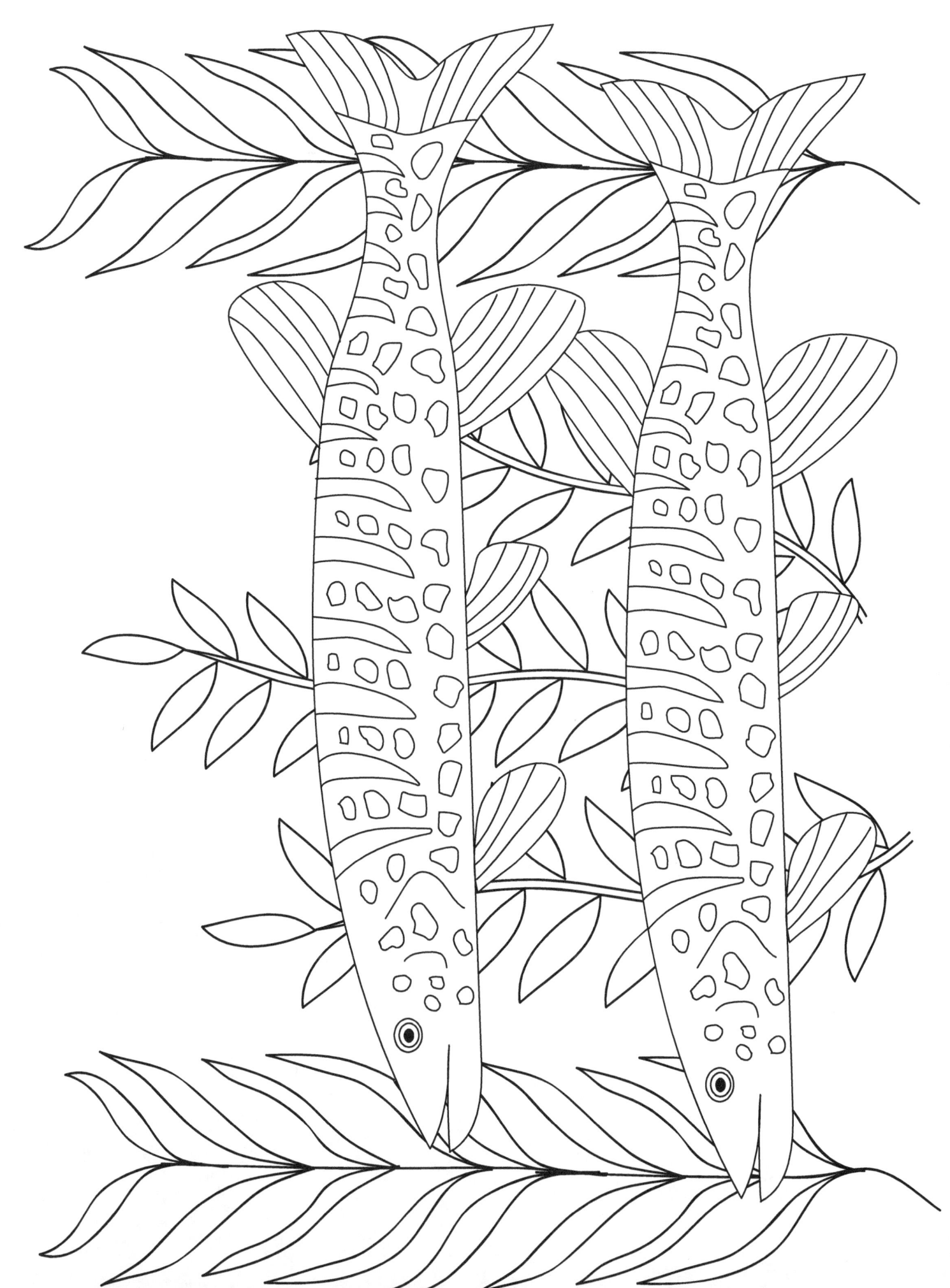

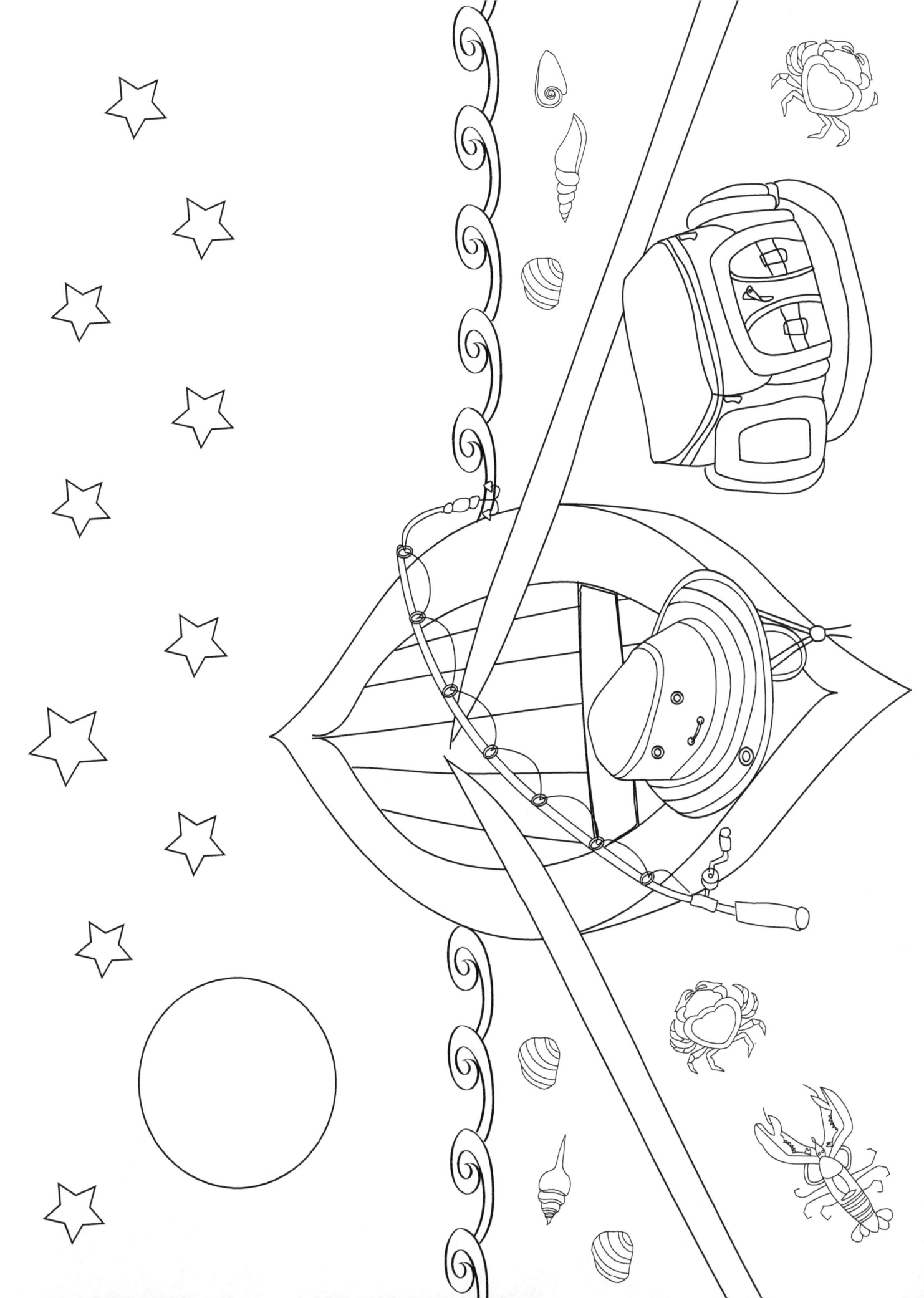

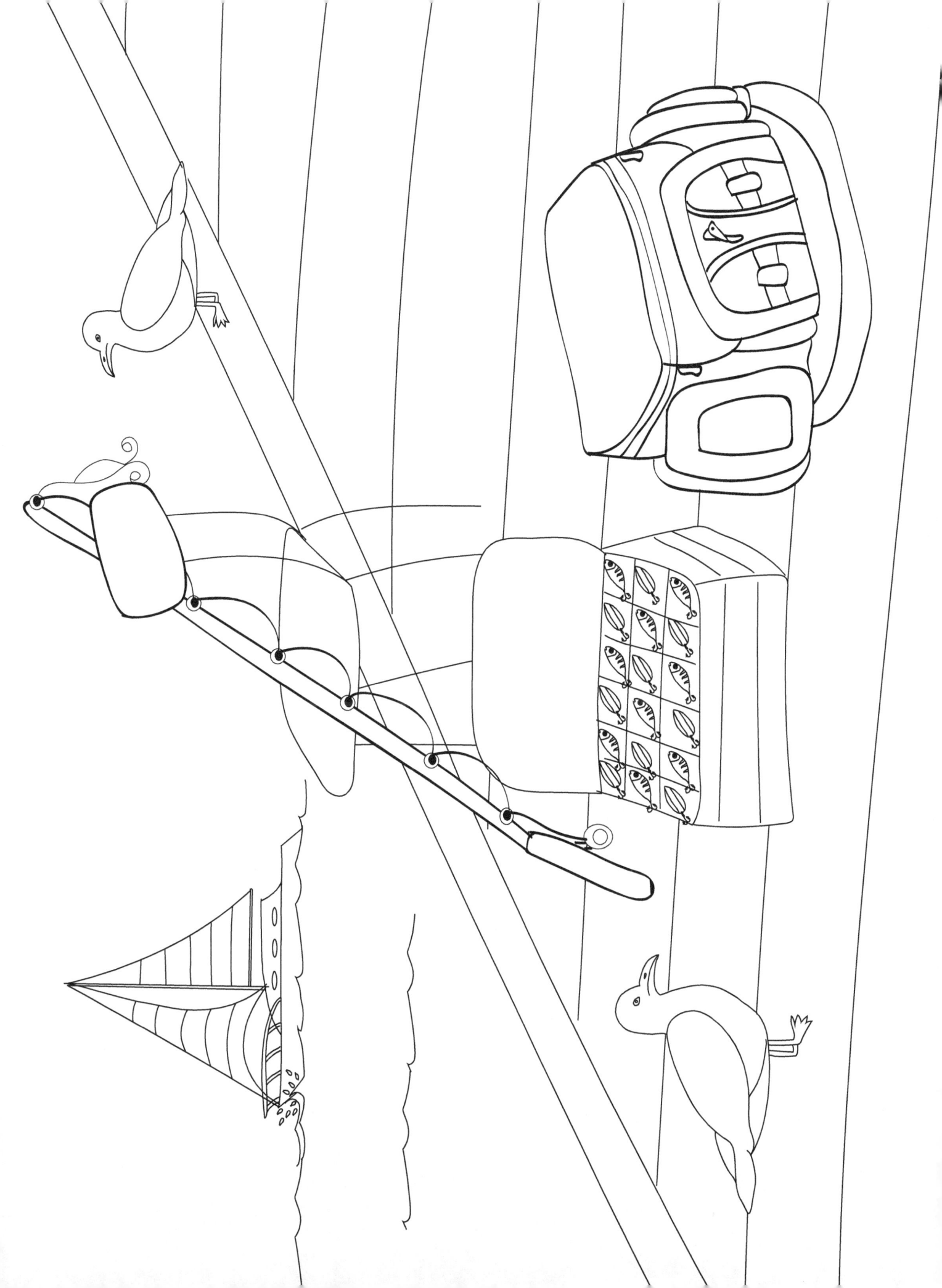

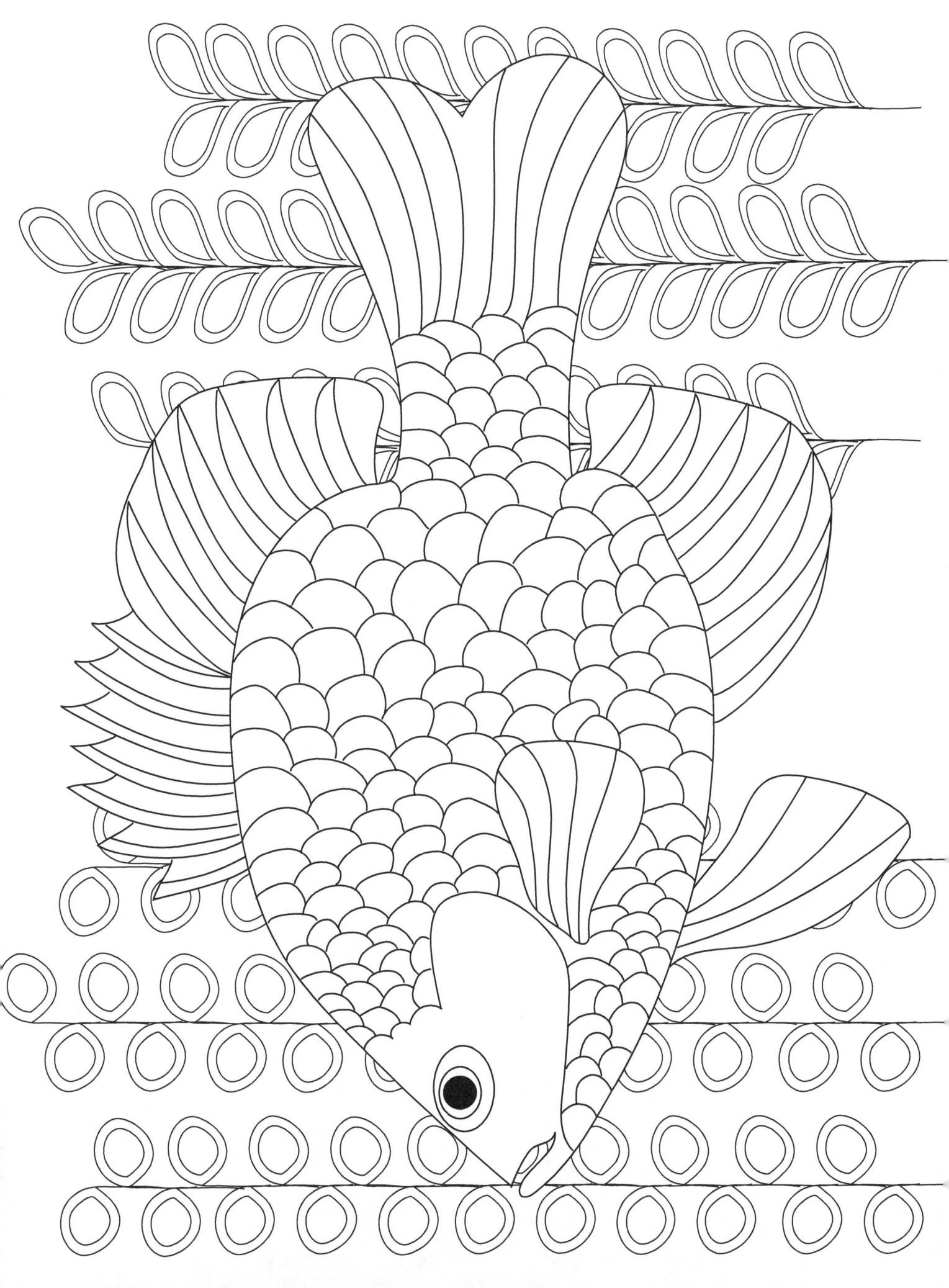

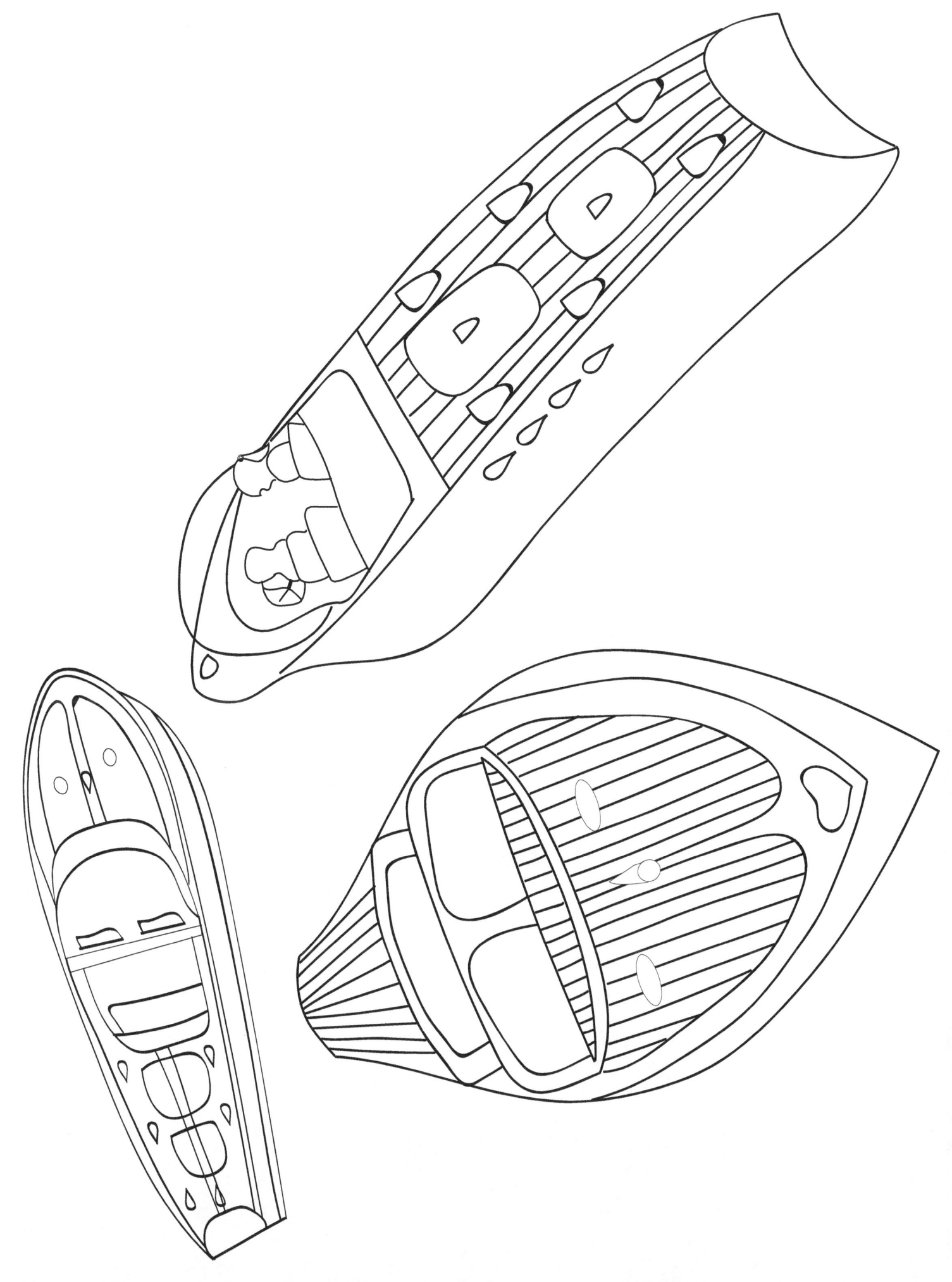

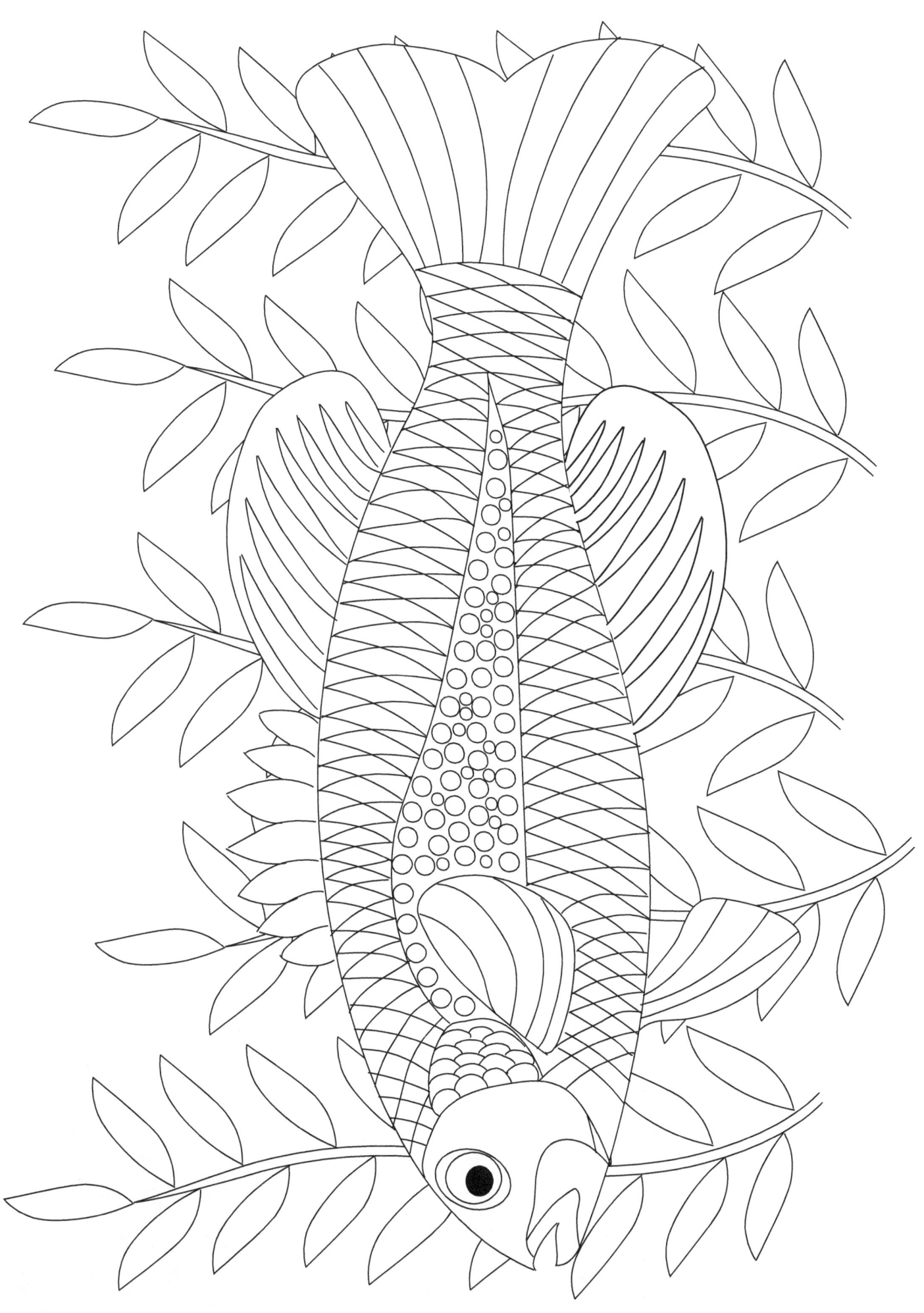

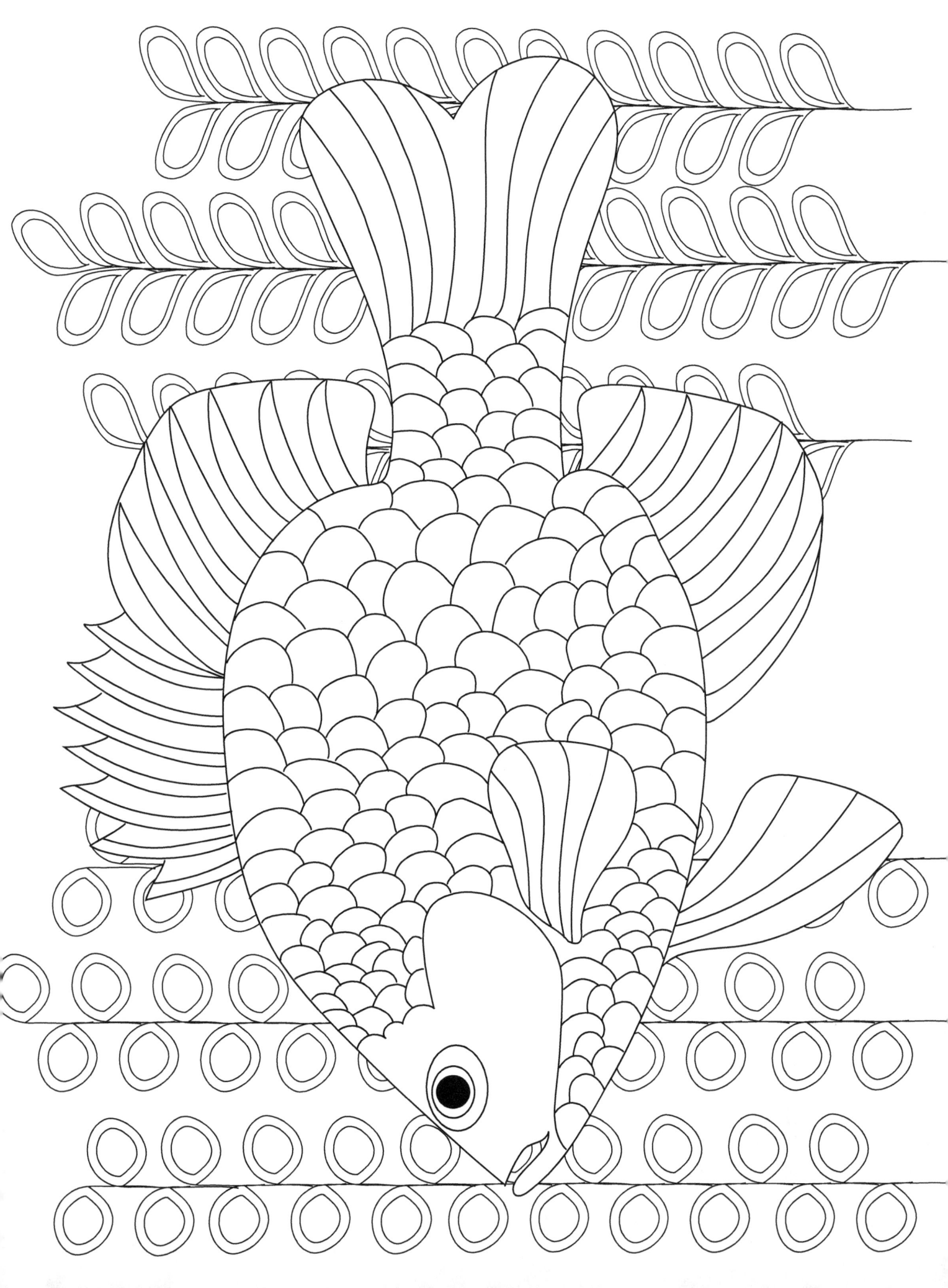

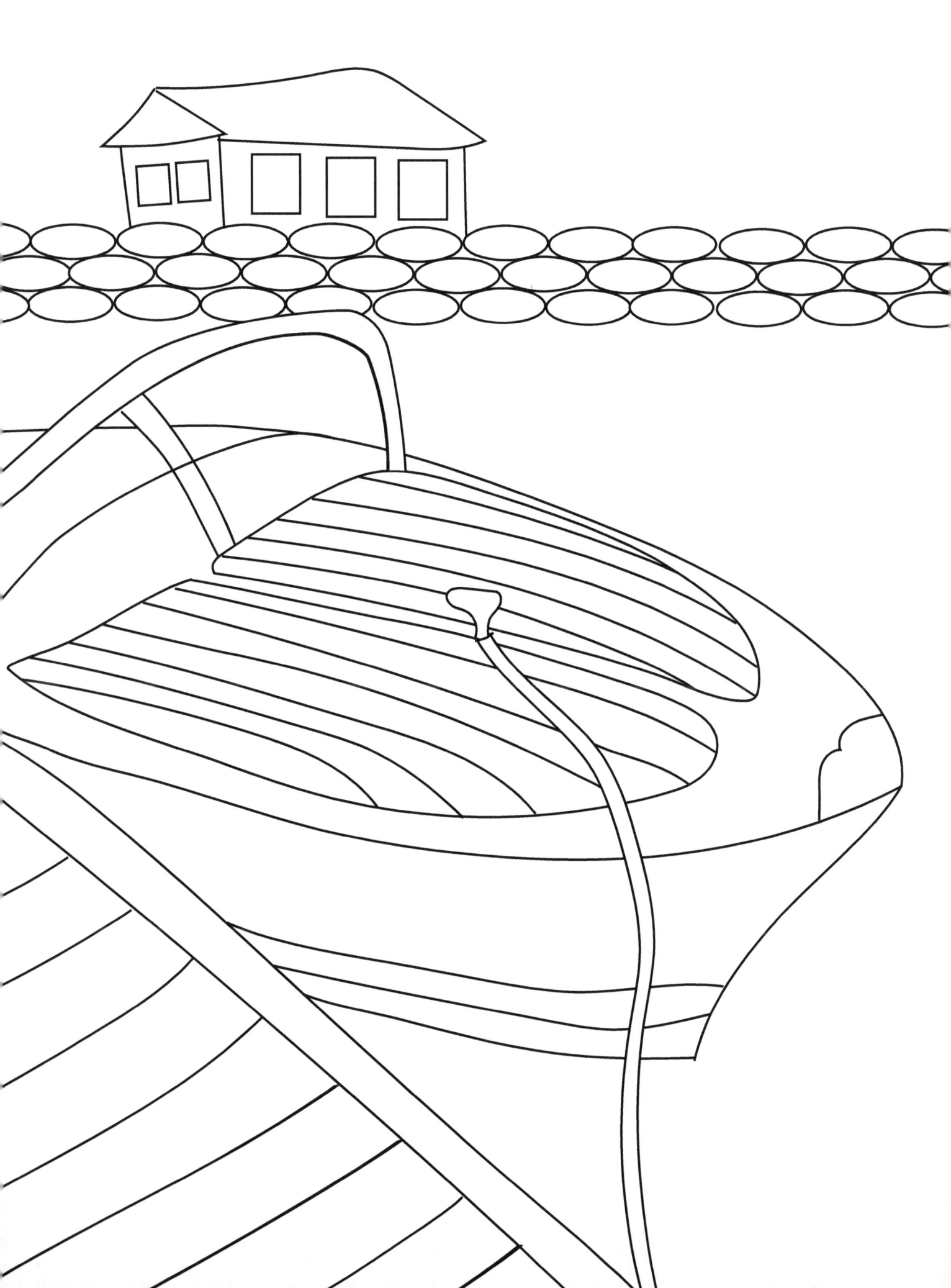

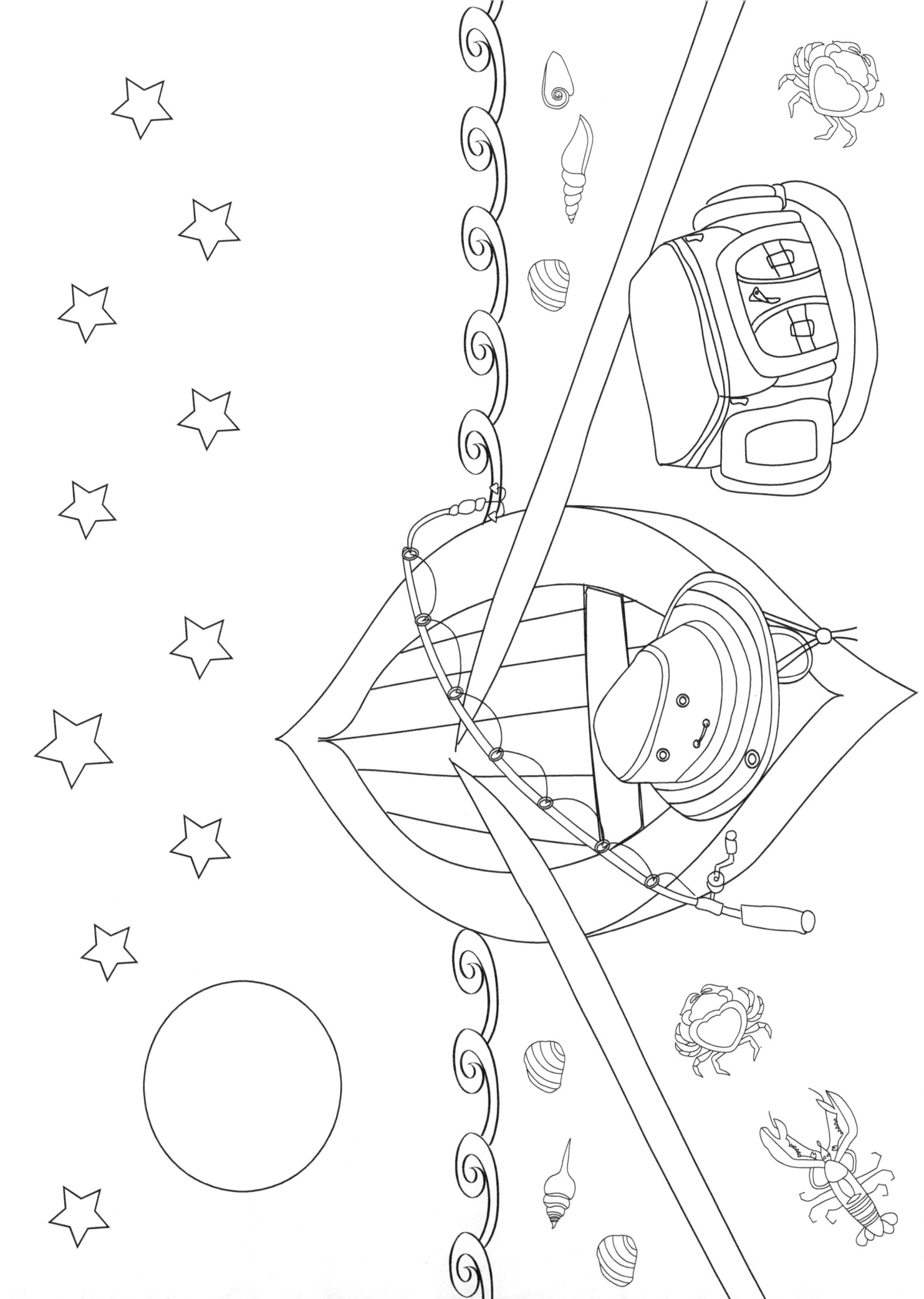

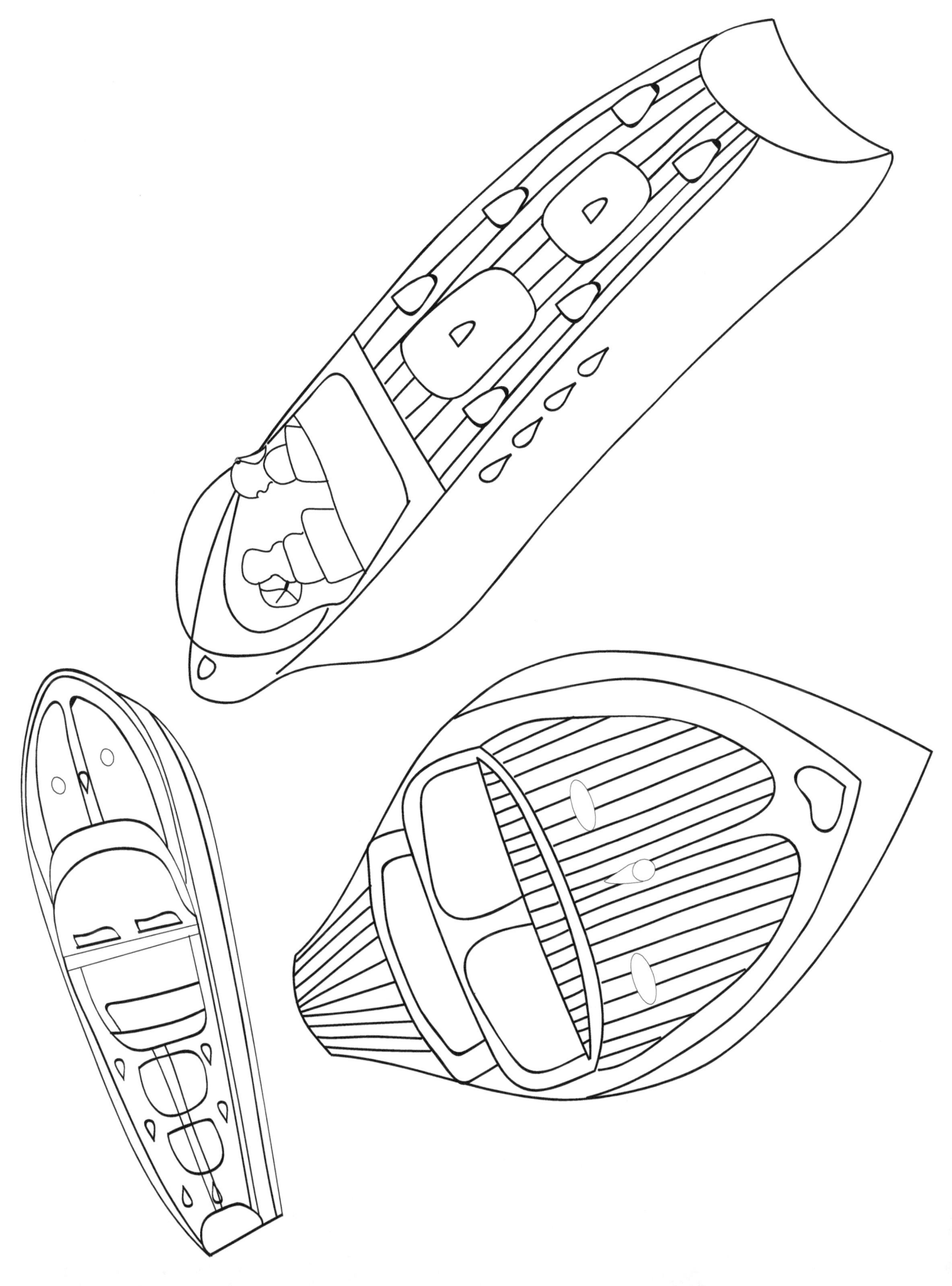

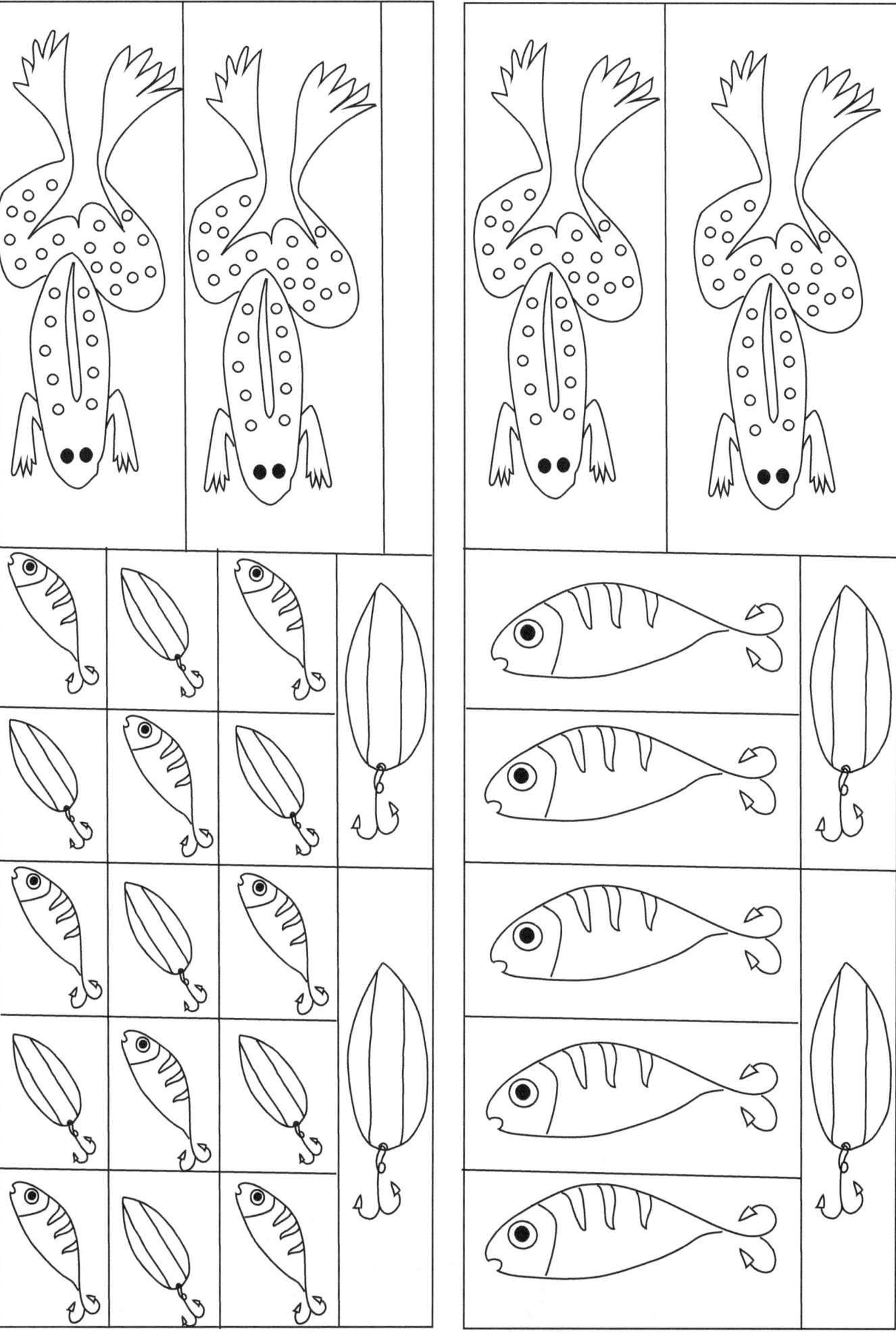

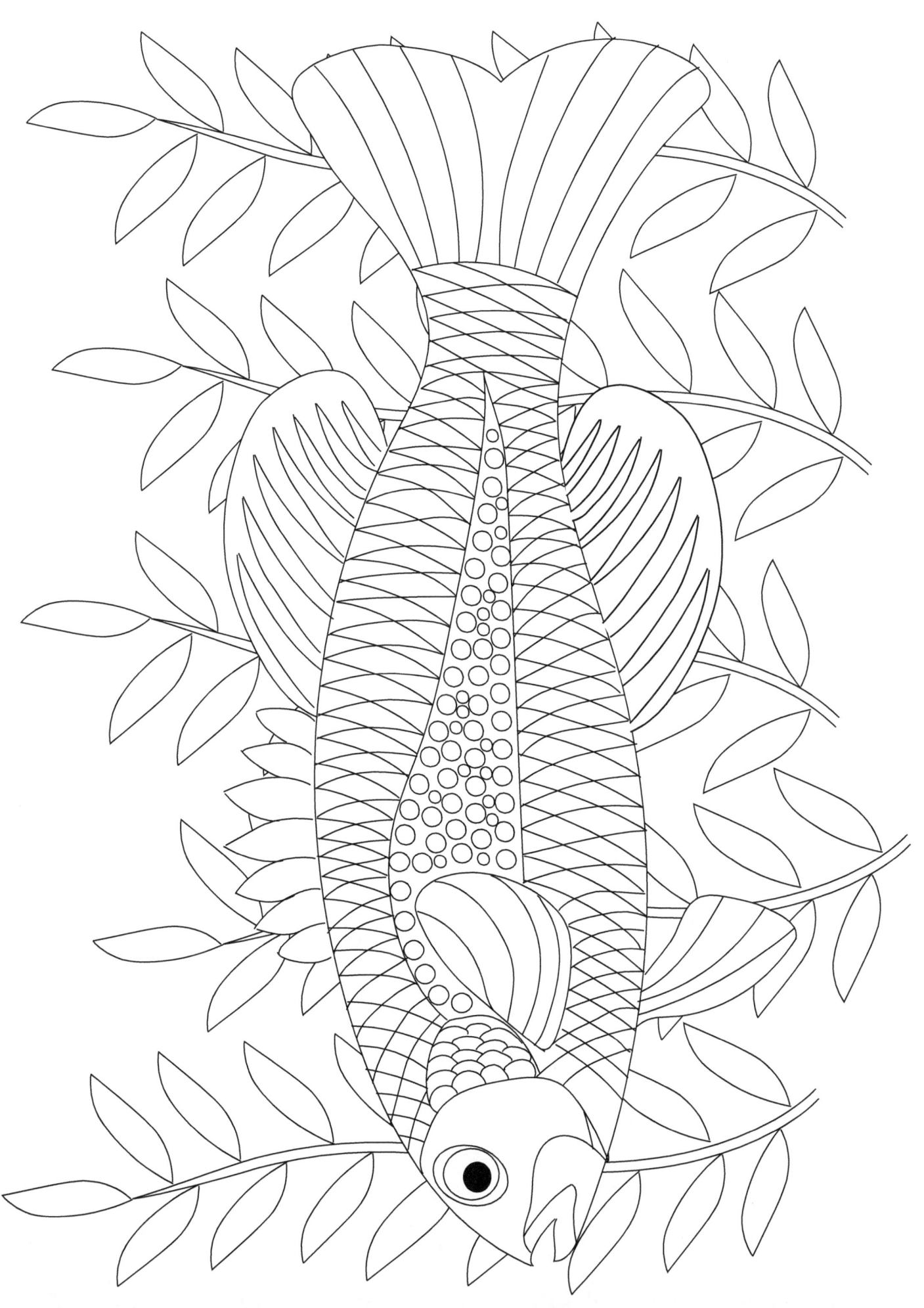

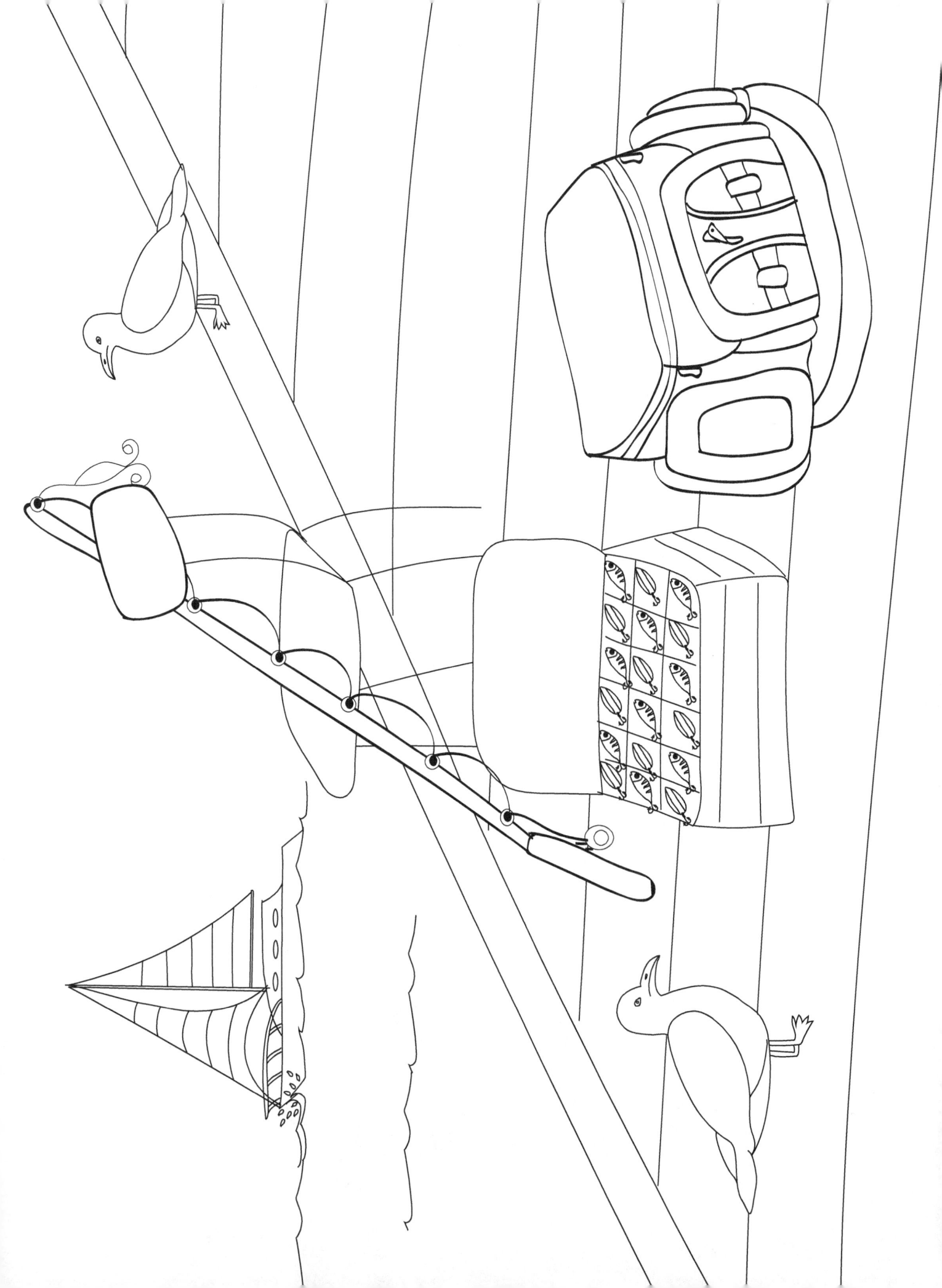

CPSIA information can be obtained
at www.ICGtesting.com
Printed in the USA
LVHW061758140420
653416LV00011B/852